# Eating the Alphabet

## Fruits and Vegetables from A to Z

# by Lois Ehlert
## Harcourt, Inc.

SAN DIEGO   NEW YORK   LONDON

TELL ME WHAT YOU EAT,

AND I WILL TELL YOU WHAT YOU ARE.

— ANTHELME BRILLAT-SAVARIN

(1755-1826)

Special thanks to Peggy Daum Judge, Food Consultant

Library of Congress Cataloging-in-Publication Data
Ehlert, Lois.
  Eating the alphabet: fruits and vegetables from
A to Z/by Lois Ehlert.
    p.  cm.
    Summary: An alphabetical tour of the world of fruits
    and vegetables, from apricot and artichoke to yam
    and zucchini.
  ISBN 0-15-224435-2    ISBN 0-15-224436-0 pb
  1. English language—Alphabet—Juvenile literature.
  2. Fruit—Juvenile literature.  3. Vegetables—Juvenile
  literature. [1. Alphabet. 2. Fruit. 3. Vegetables.] I. Title.
  PE1155.E35   1989
  [E]—dc19       88-10906

Display and text type set in Century Schoolbook
Printed and bound by Tien Wah Press, Singapore

V U T S R

Printed in Singapore

More books by Lois Ehlert

*A sembrar sopa de verduras*
*Cuckoo/Cucú: A Mexican Folktale/*
  *Un cuento folklórico mexicano*
*Feathers for Lunch*
*Fish Eyes: A Book You Can Count On*
*Growing Vegetable Soup*
*Hands*
*Mole's Hill*
*Moon Rope/Un lazo a la luna*
*Nuts to You!*
*Planting a Rainbow*
*Plumas para almorzar*
*Red Leaf, Yellow Leaf*
*Snowballs*

Apple to Zucchini,
come take a look.
Start eating your way
through this alphabet book.

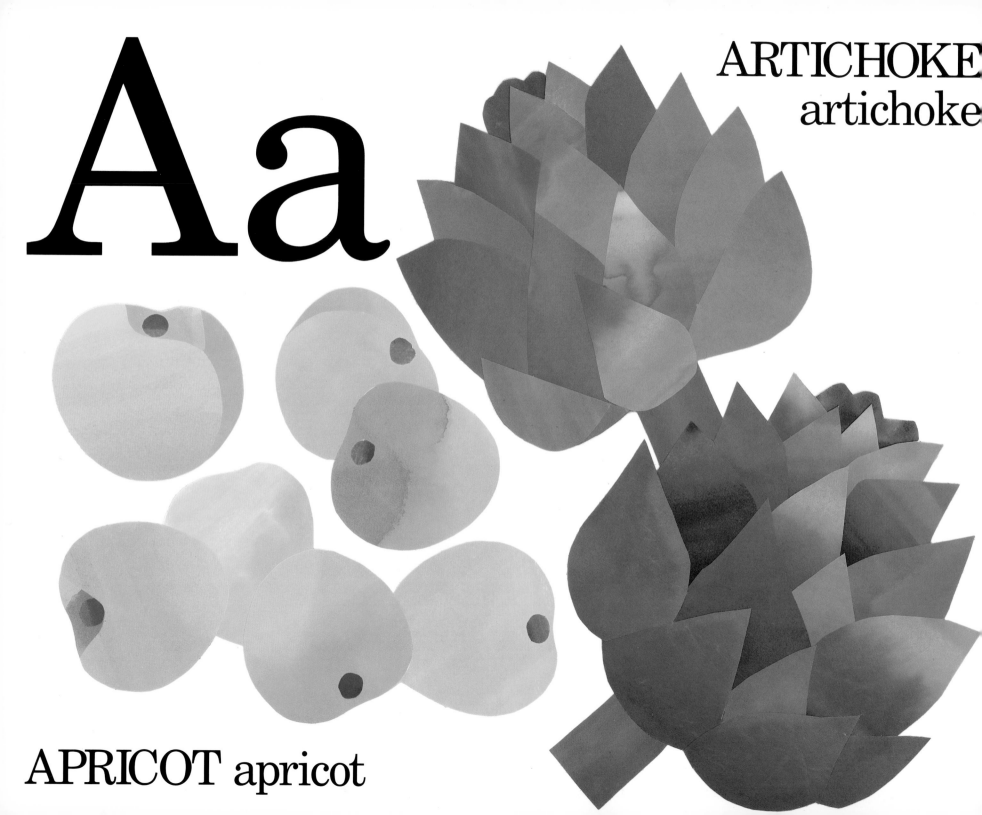

# Aa

ARTICHOKE artichoke

APRICOT apricot

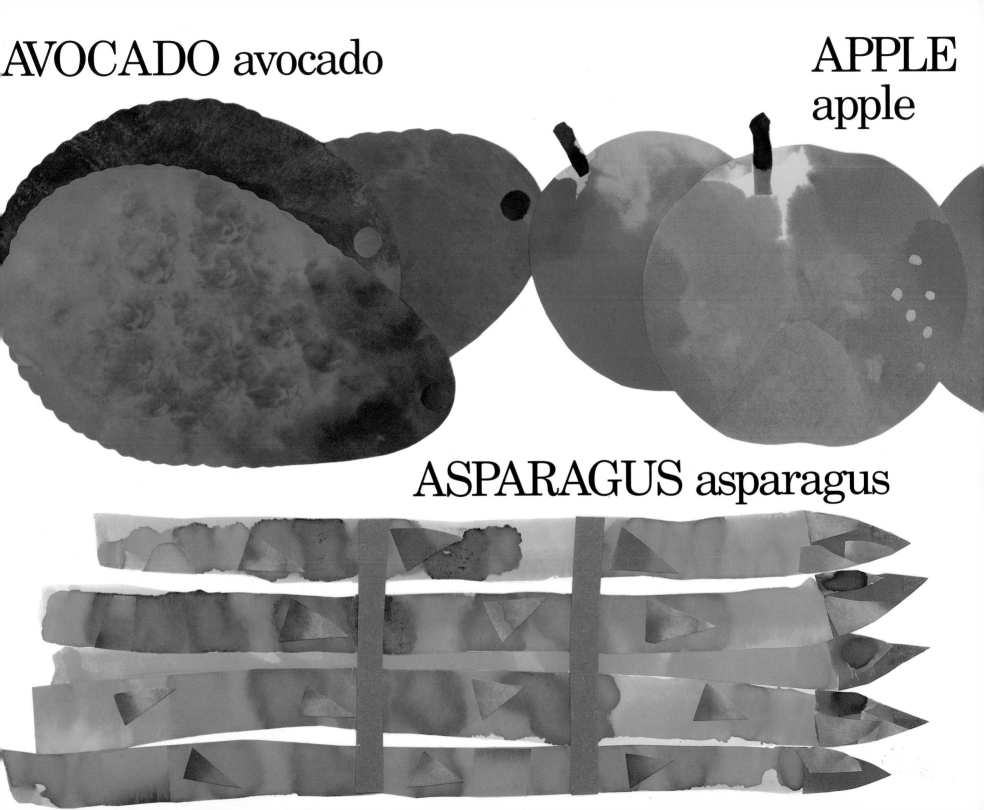

AVOCADO avocado

APPLE apple

ASPARAGUS asparagus

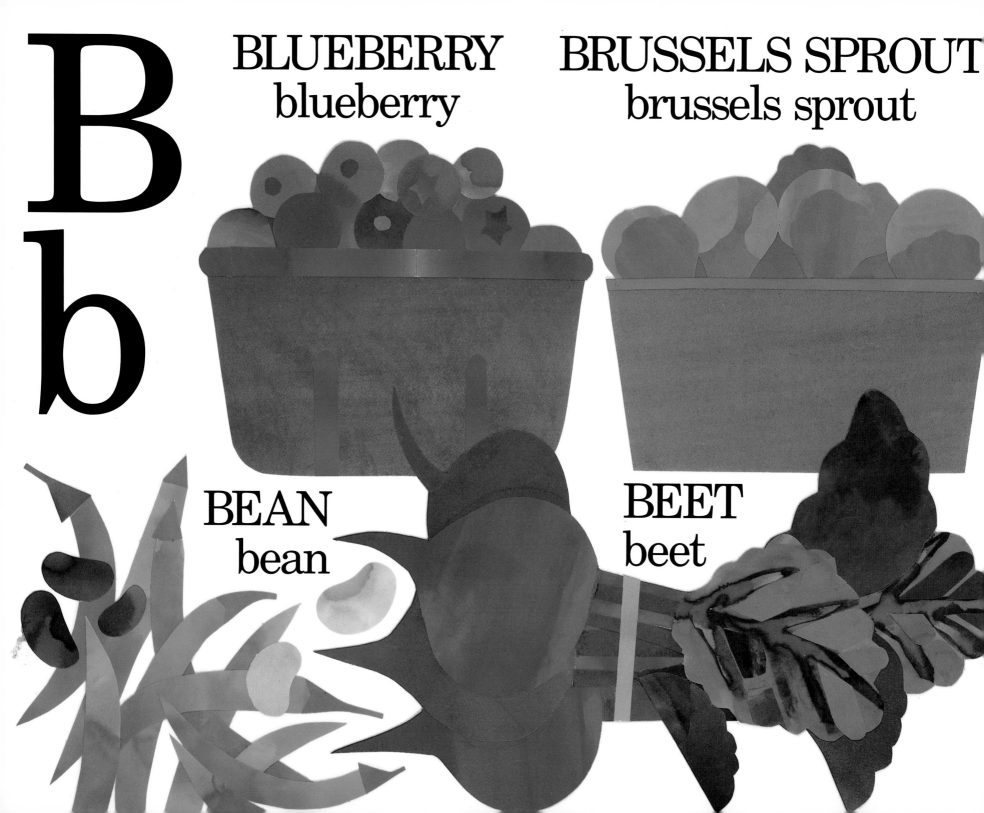

# B b

**BLUEBERRY**
blueberry

**BRUSSELS SPROUT**
brussels sprout

**BEAN**
bean

**BEET**
beet

BANANA
banana

BROCCOLI
broccoli

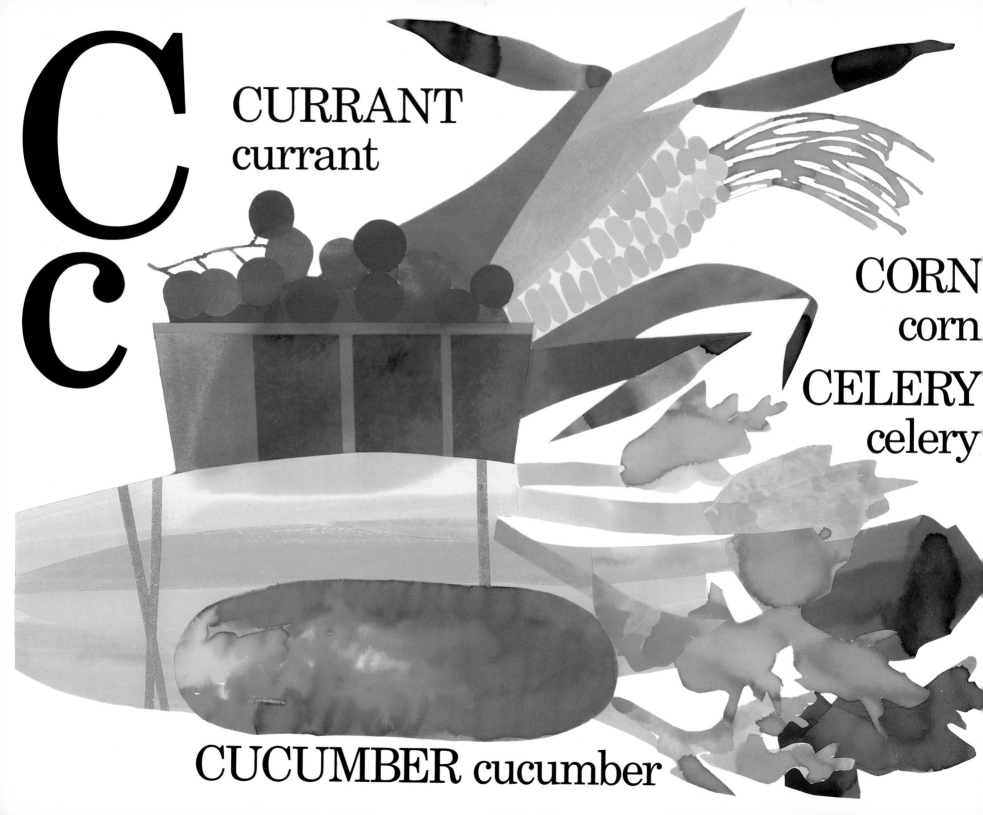

C c

CURRANT
currant

CORN
corn

CELERY
celery

CUCUMBER cucumber

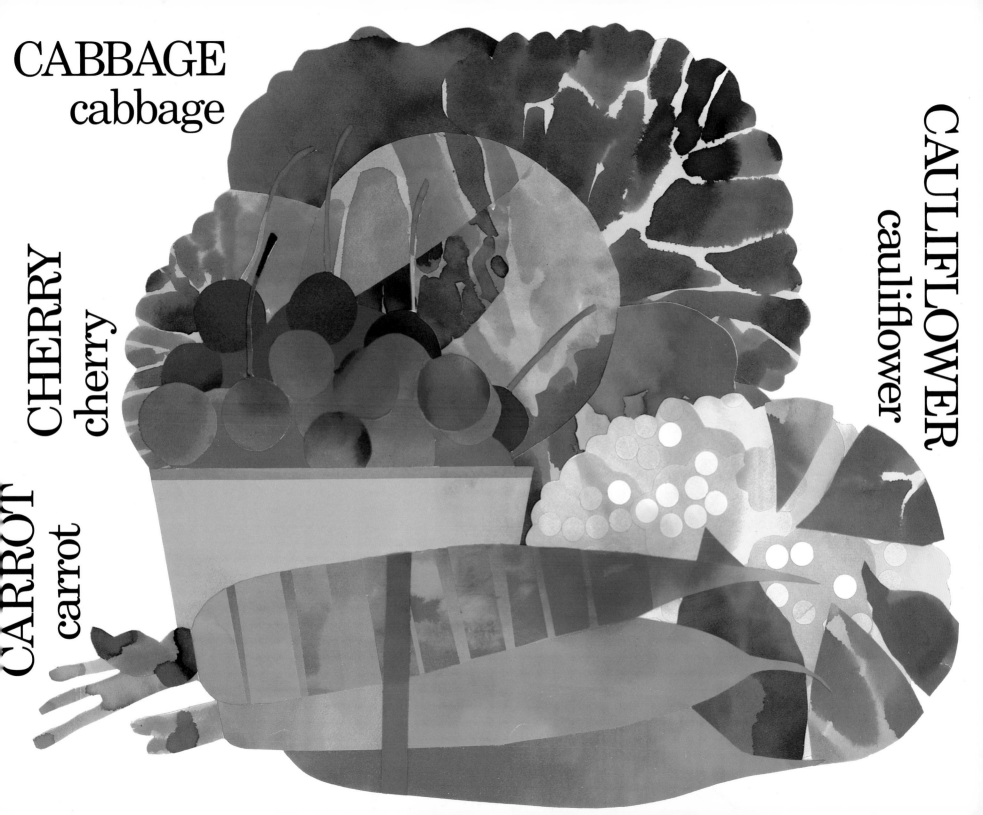

CABBAGE
cabbage

CAULIFLOWER
cauliflower

CHERRY
cherry

CARROT
carrot

# Dd  Ee

DATE
date

ENDIVE
endive

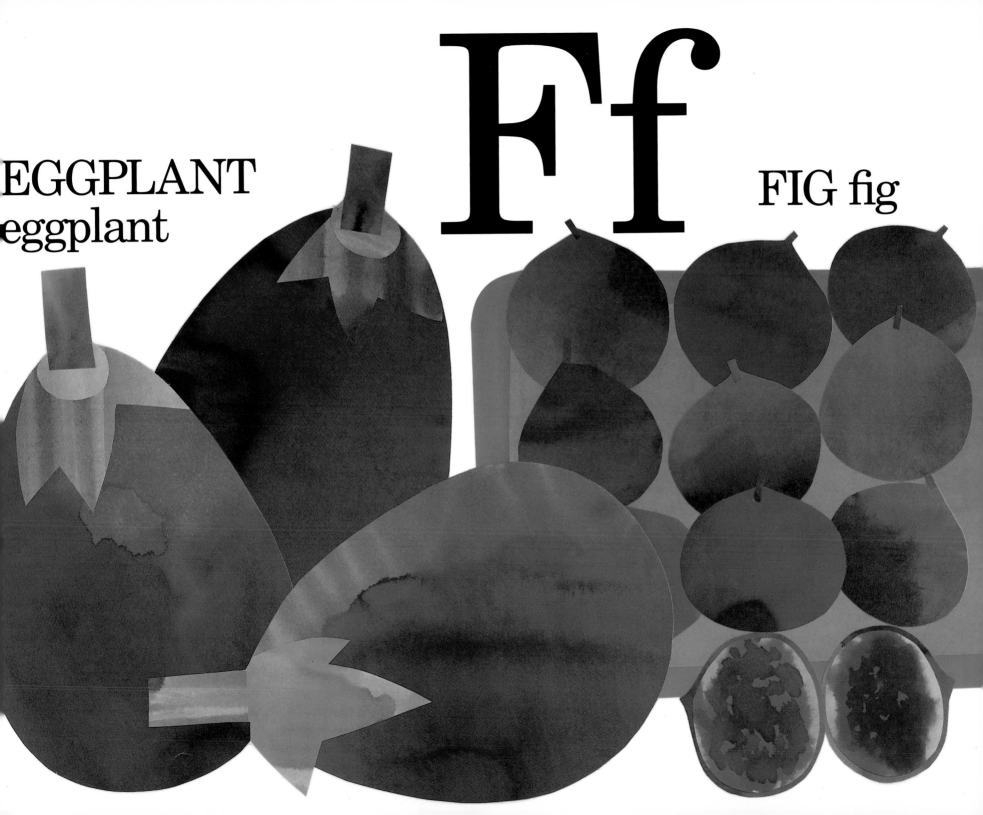

EGGPLANT
eggplant

Ff

FIG fig

# Gg

## GOOSEBERRY
### gooseberry

## GRAPEFRUIT
### grapefruit

GRAPES
grapes

# Hh

HUCKLEBERRY
huckleberry

# Ii

## INDIAN CORN
### Indian corn

# Jj

## JALAPEÑO
### jalapeño

## JICAMA
### jicama

# K k

KUMQUAT kumquat

KIWIFRUIT kiwifruit

KOHLRABI kohlrabi

# Ll

LEEK
leek

LEMON
lemon

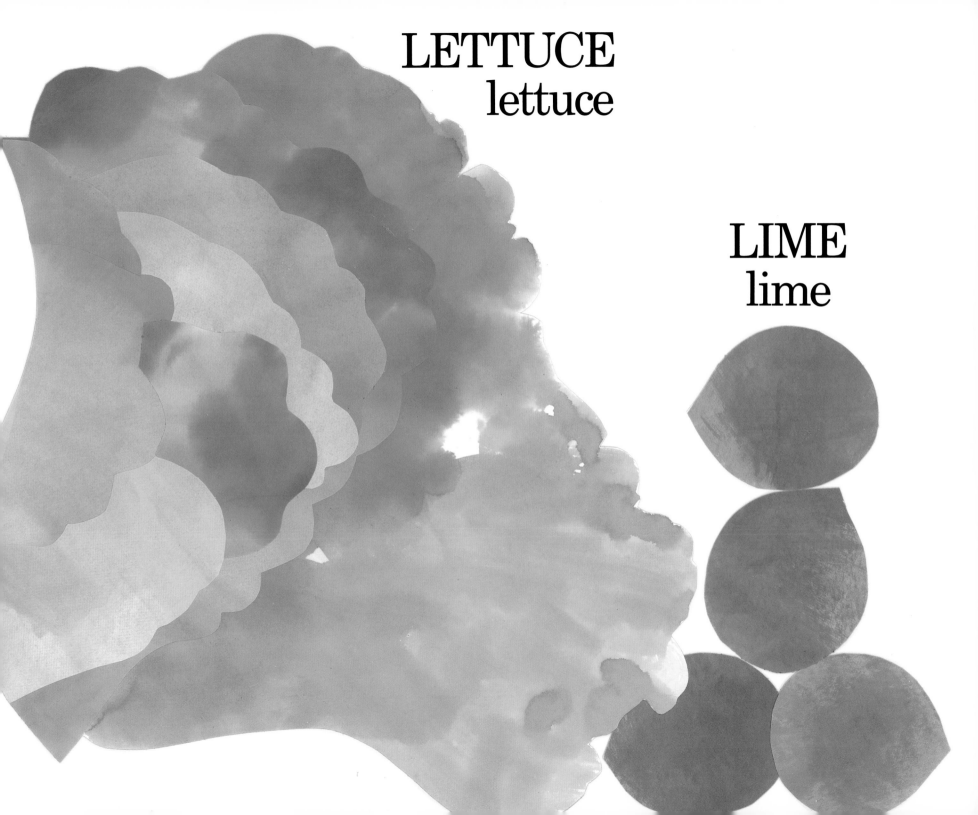

LETTUCE
lettuce

LIME
lime

# Mm

MANGO mango

# Nn

MELON melon

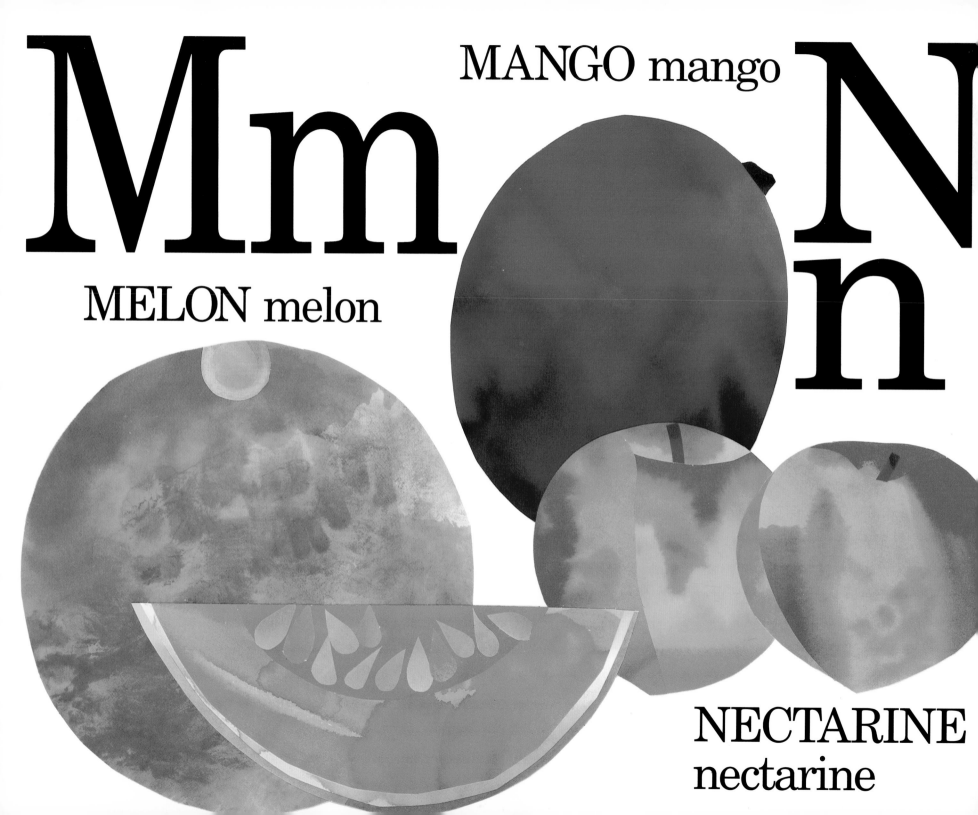

NECTARINE
nectarine

# O o

ORANGE
orange

OKRA
okra

ONION
onion

# P p

PINEAPPLE
pineapple

PEACH
peach

PEAR
pear

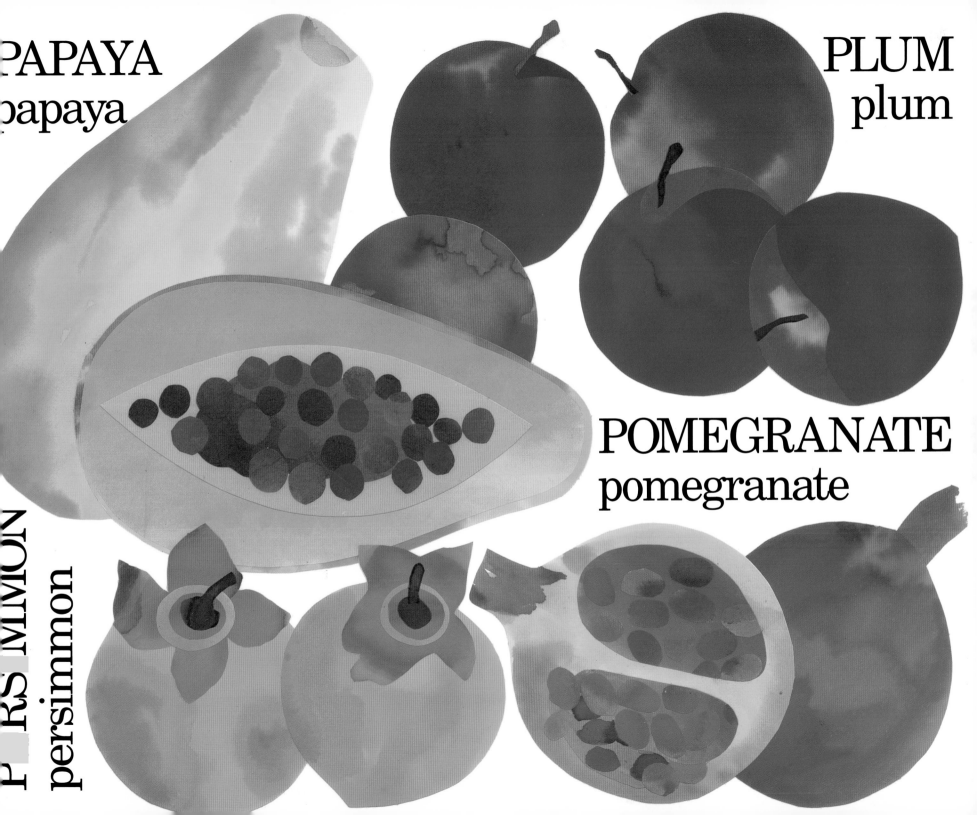

PAPAYA
papaya

PLUM
plum

POMEGRANATE
pomegranate

PERSIMMON
persimmon

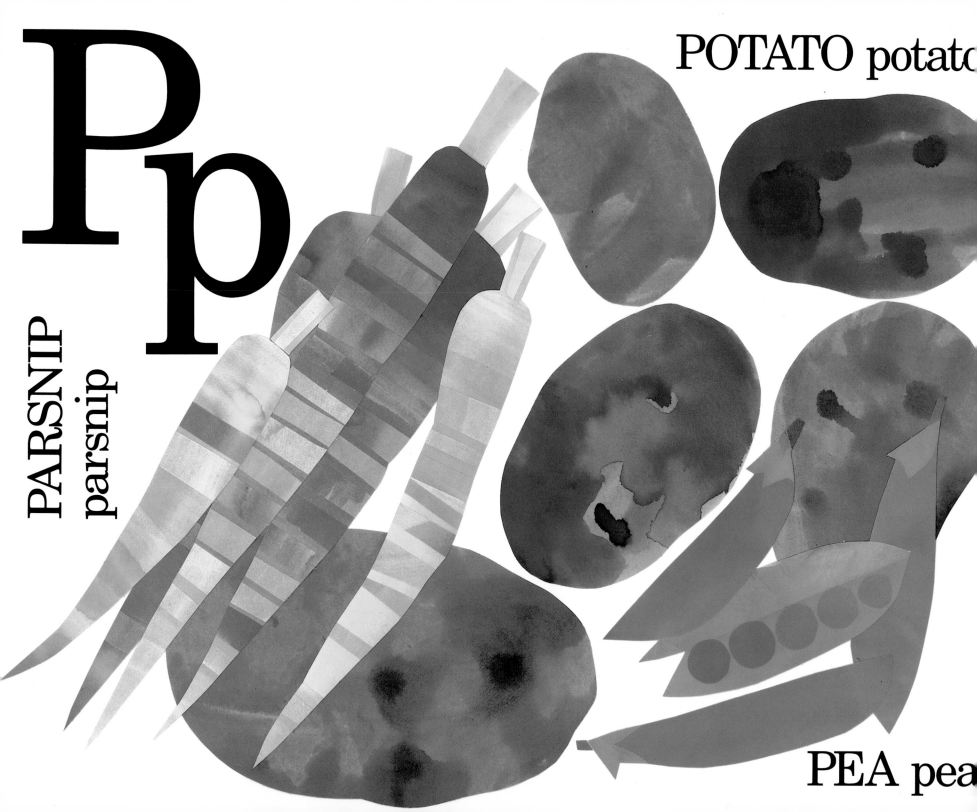

# Pp

PARSNIP parsnip

POTATO potato

PEA pea

PUMPKIN
pumpkin

PEPPER
pepper

# Qq Rr

RUTABAGA
rutabaga

QUINCE
quince

RASPBERRY
raspberry

RADISH
radish

RADICCHIO
radicchio

RHUBARB rhubarb

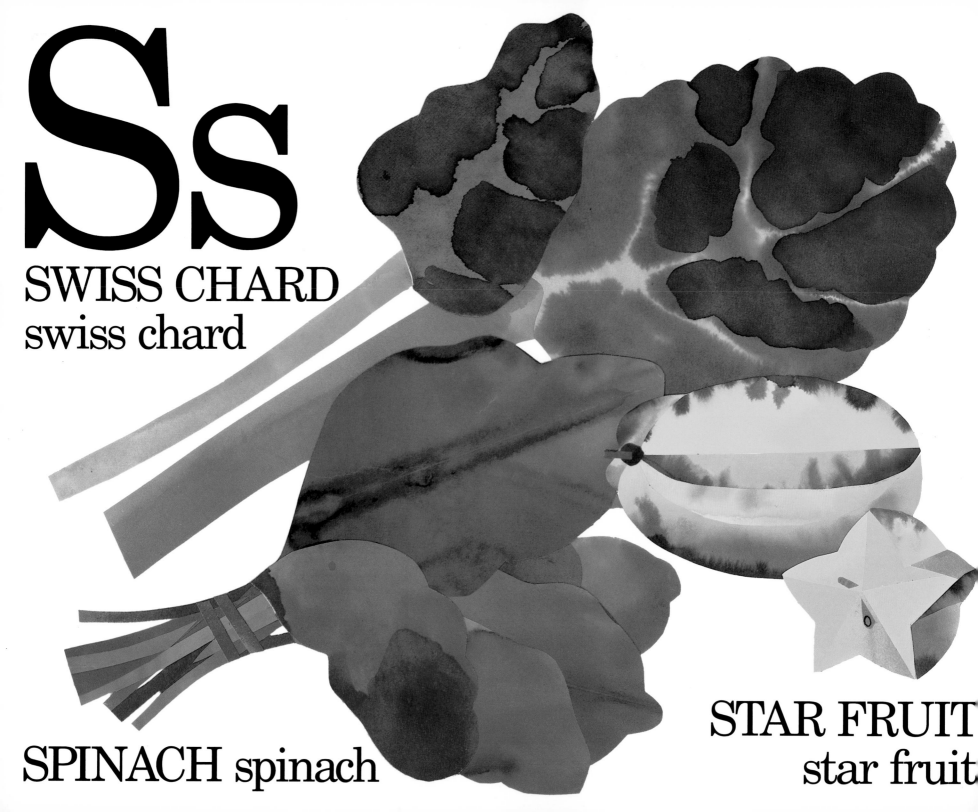

# Ss

SWISS CHARD
swiss chard

SPINACH spinach

STAR FRUIT
star fruit

STRAWBERRY
strawberry

Tt

TURNIP
turnip

TANGERINE
tangerine

TOMATO tomato

# Uu

# Vv

UGLI FRUIT ugli fruit

VEGETABLE MARROW vegetable marrow

# Ww

WATERCRESS

watercress

WATERMELON watermelon

# Xx
### XIGUA xigua

# Yy
### YAM yam

# Zz
### ZUCCHINI zucchini

To learn more about the fruits and vegetables in this book, turn the page.

# Glossary of Fruits and Vegetables in This Book

**A** APPLE (APP-uhl) *fruit*
Thought to be the forbidden fruit of the Bible, the apple has been grown for at least six thousand years. It is the most widely grown fruit of temperate areas. It grows on a tree and may be red, yellow, or green when ripe.

APRICOT (AY-prih-kott or APP-rih-kott) *fruit*
The apricot is probably native to China and has grown in central Asia and Europe for centuries. The peachlike, plum-sized fruit grows on a tree.

ARTICHOKE (AHR-tih-chohwk) *vegetable*
The artichoke is native to the Mediterranean area. Also called globe artichoke, it is the unopened flower head of a thistlelike plant. It is not related to jerusalem artichoke, the tuber of another plant.

ASPARAGUS (as-PAIR-ah-guss) *vegetable*
Asparagus may have originated in the Mediterranean area and now grows in most temperate and subtropical areas. Individual stalks, which grow out of the ground, are one of the first vegetables of spring.

AVOCADO (av-oh-CAH-doh) *fruit/vegetable*
The avocado grows on a tree that is native to Mexico and Central and South America. It is also called alligator pear. Although it is a fruit, it is often thought to be a vegetable.

**B** BANANA (bah-NANN-ah) *fruit*
The banana, probably native to Asia, was known in India four thousand years ago. It grows in a cluster on a treelike plant. Because it grows year-round, it is one of the world's most popular and important crops.

BEAN (beeen) *vegetable*
The bean has been grown throughout the world since prehistoric times. The seed (dried bean) or seed pod (string bean) grows on a plant. Some dried beans are lima and kidney. The wax bean is a yellow string bean.

BEET (beeet) *vegetable*
The beet, a cultivated version of a plant that grew wild in the Mediterranean area, now is grown throughout Europe and North America. It is an edible root. The young green leaves can be eaten as well.

BLUEBERRY (BLOO-behr-ee) *fruit*
The blueberry first was a wild North American berry. It grows on a shrub. Native Americans taught settlers how to dry the berries for use all winter long.

BROCCOLI (BRAHK-uh-lee) *vegetable*
Broccoli is native to the eastern Mediterranean area and Asia Minor. It is related to cabbage and cauliflower and grows on a plant. The floweret is a cluster of green buds picked and eaten before the flowers open.

BRUSSELS SPROUT (BRUSS-uhlz SPROWT) *vegetable*
Native to Europe, this vegetable is a type of miniature cabbage. Sprouts cluster along the stalk of the plant.

**C** CABBAGE (KAB-ihj) *vegetable*
Cabbage grew in Europe and probably Asia in prehistoric times. Now it grows in temperate areas throughout the world. There are many types, both green and red. The cabbage head grows in the center of the plant.

CARROT (KAIR-uht) *vegetable*
The carrot is native to Europe and was cultivated in the Mediterranean area two thousand years ago. Now it grows in many temperate areas and is very popular in the United States. It is an edible root.

CAULIFLOWER (KAW-lih-flouw-uhr) *vegetable*
Cauliflower probably developed in Europe and the Middle East. The compact head, which is partially developed flowers, grows in the center of the plant.

CELERY (SELL-uhr-ee) *vegetable*
Celery is native to the Mediterranean area and the Middle East and was cultivated by the Romans. Related to the carrot, it has a stalk that grows aboveground.

CHERRY (CHAIR-ee) *fruit*
The cherry is probably native to western Asia and eastern Europe. Now it grows in almost all temperate areas. There are three types: sweet (often dark), for eating; sour (often bright red), for baking pies and other dishes; and sweet-sour hybrids.

CORN (korrn) *vegetable*
Corn, native to the Americas, has been used as food for almost ten thousand years. It is also called sweet corn or maize. The corn kernel is a seed, grown on "ears" on a tall plant. Corn is a very important grain crop.

CUCUMBER (QUEW-kuhm-buhr) *fruit/vegetable*
Native to southern Asia, the cucumber was known in the Thailand area nearly twelve thousand years ago. Related to squash, it is a vine fruit that is considered a vegetable.

CURRANT (KUHR-ant) *fruit*
The tart currant berry was cultivated around the Baltic Sea. Popular in Europe and the United States, it grows on a shrub. Red, black, or white, it is often used to make jelly.

**D** DATE (dayt) *fruit*
The date, which has been known since prehistoric times, came from the Middle East and northern Africa. Now it also is grown in California and Arizona. It grows on the date palm tree and is often dried.

**E** EGGPLANT (EHG-plant) *fruit/vegetable*
Eggplant is probably native to India. It has been grown in Asia since ancient times on a plantlike bush. It can be purple, white, or yellow. White eggplants look like eggs. Really a fruit, it is considered a vegetable.

ENDIVE (EHN-dyv or AHN-deev) *vegetable*
Endive probably came from southern Asia or Egypt. It is an herb plant with curly, edible leaves. Sometimes called chicory, it has a sharper flavor than most salad greens.

**F** FIG (fihg) *fruit*
The fig is native to Asia Minor. It was one of the first cultivated fruits. It is now grown throughout the Mediterranean and in California. It grows on a bush or small tree and is often dried.

**G** GOOSEBERRY (GOOZ-behr-ee) *fruit*
The gooseberry is probably native to northern Europe. It is related to the currant and can be green, white, yellow, or red. It grows on a shrub. Very tart, it is often used to make jam and pastry.

GRAPE (grayp) *fruit*
The grape, known in ancient times, is probably native to western Asia. It grows in a cluster on a vine. Seedless types have been developed. The raisin is a dried grape.

GRAPEFRUIT (GRAYP-froot) *fruit*
The grapefruit is a relatively new fruit. It probably originated in the West Indies in the 1700s as a new variety of the pomelo, a coarser citrus fruit. It grows on a tree in grapelike clusters. The tart pulp can be white or pink.

**H** HUCKLEBERRY (HUHK-uhl-behr-ee) *fruit*
The shiny, blue-black huckleberry, native to North America, grows on a shrub. It is related to the blueberry but is larger. Inside are ten hard seeds.

**I** INDIAN CORN (INN-dih-an KORRN) *vegetable*
Indian corn grows on "ears" that develop on a tall plant, a type of Native American cereal grass. Indian corn is dried, not eaten fresh. The dried kernels are ground and used as grain. (*See also* corn.)

**J** JALAPEÑO (hah-lah-PAY-nyoh) *fruit/vegetable*
The jalapeño is a hot pepper, probably native to Mexico. It grows on a plant. The jalapeño makes food spicy. Note: Wash your hands after cutting a jalapeño, or you'll cry if you touch your eyes. (*See also* pepper.)

JICAMA (HEE-cah-mah) *vegetable*
The jicama is native to Mexico and Central and South America and later became popular in the Orient. It is a tuberous root—a thick, fleshy storage root that grows underground. It is turnip-shaped, white inside, and has a sweet, crunchy taste.

**K** KIWIFRUIT (KEE-wee-froot) *fruit*
Kiwifruit is probably native to China and was developed in New Zealand in the early 1900s. Fuzzy like the kiwi bird, it grows on a vine. Another name for it is Chinese gooseberry.

KOHLRABI (kohwl-RAH-bee) *vegetable*
Kohlrabi originated in Europe. Related to cabbage, kohlrabi is the enlarged part of a stem, growing partly aboveground. It can be white or purple. The young, tender leaves can be eaten as well.

KUMQUAT (KUHM-kwaht) *fruit*
The kumquat is native to eastern Asia, probably China. Something like a tart miniature orange, it grows on a small tree. It is often preserved whole or used to make jam. The thin rind is edible.

**L** LEEK (leeek) *vegetable*
In ancient times the leek was grown in the Near East. It grows as an underground bulb. Part of the onion family, it looks like a large green onion but has a milder flavor.

LEMON (LEHM-uhn) *fruit*
The lemon, probably native to India, grows on a small, thorny tree. The oval citrus fruit is very tart. The juice, when sweetened, makes refreshing lemonade.

LETTUCE (LEHT-ihs or LEHT-uhs) *vegetable*
Lettuce, native to the Mediterranean area, is a member of the chicory family. Its leaves may be tight (head lettuce) or loose (leaf lettuce). There are many popular varieties of lettuce.

LIME (lym) *fruit*
The lime probably originated in southeastern Asia. It grows on a small tree. Smaller than a lemon, it is also tart but has its own special flavor.

**M** MANGO (MANG-goh) *fruit*
The mango, native to tropical areas of Asia, was probably cultivated approximately four thousand years ago. The oval fruit grows on a tree. Firm but juicy, it tastes like a spicy peach. Some call it "king of the tropical fruits."

MELON (MEHL-uhn) *fruit*
The melon is native to central Asia, and it grows on a vine. There are many different types. Some melons, like cantaloupe, have orange flesh, and some, like honeydew, have green flesh.

**N** NECTARINE (nehk-teh-REEN) *fruit*
The nectarine, known for more than two thousand years, grows in many temperate areas. Closely related to the peach, it has been called a fuzzless peach because of its smooth skin. Like a peach, it grows on a tree.

**O** OKRA (OH-krah) *fruit/vegetable*
Okra, native to Africa, grows on a tall plant. The small, unripe pod is eaten. When cooked, the pod gives out a sticky juice that thickens liquids. Sometimes okra is called gumbo, the name used for okra stew.

ONION (UHN-yuhn) *vegetable*
The onion, native to central or southwestern Asia, is part of the lily family. The edible bulb grows underground. It can be yellow, white, or red. The green onion, or scallion, is a young onion picked early.

ORANGE (OHR-inj) *fruit*
The orange, one of the oldest cultivated fruits, probably originated in southwestern Asia. It grows on a tree and is really a berry. Some oranges are sour.

**P** PAPAYA (pah-PY-ah) *fruit*
The papaya is native to the Central American region. The oblong fruit, firm but juicy, grows on a large, palmlike plant. It has spicy black seeds that can be eaten.

PARSNIP (PAHR-snipp) *vegetable*
The parsnip, native to northern Europe, has been known for two thousand years. A member of the carrot family, it is an edible root that looks like a white carrot. If it stays in the ground over winter, it is sweeter in spring.

PEA (peee) *vegetable*
The pea, one of the oldest cultivated vegetables, was known in southeastern Asia nearly twelve thousand years ago. It grows in all temperate areas. The pea is a seed inside a pod on a vine. In new varieties, both pea and pod are tender.

PEACH (peeech) *fruit*
The peach probably originated in China at least four thousand years ago. Now it grows in temperate climates throughout the world. It grows on a tree. The sweet, juicy flesh is a covering for the hard seed, or pit, inside.

PEAR (pair) *fruit*
The pear is probably of European origin and has grown in Asia for more than two thousand years. Related to the apple, it grows on a tree. New to the United States is the crunchy Asian pear.

PEPPER (PEHP-uhr) *fruit/vegetable*
Native to the tropical Americas, the pepper can be traced back to prehistoric times. It is a podlike fruit commonly considered a vegetable. Peppers can be red, yellow, green, or purple. Hot peppers are often dried. (*See also* jalapeño.)

PERSIMMON (puhr-SIMM-uhn) *fruit*
The persimmon is native to China and Japan. The American persimmon grows wild and is native to the southern United States. The fruit grows on a tree. Persimmon pudding was a favorite Early American dessert.

PINEAPPLE (PYN-app-uhl) *fruit*
The pineapple originated in the tropical Americas. It grows on a plant and was given its name because it looks like a pine cone. The pineapple is a dense flower head.

PLUM (pluhm) *fruit*
The plum probably originated in the Middle East near the Caspian Sea. It grows on a small tree and is related to the cherry and peach. It can be red, purple, or yellow-green. Some varieties are dried as prunes.

POMEGRANATE (PAHM-a-gran-it) *fruit*
The pomegranate is probably native to Persia. It is named in ancient myths and the Old Testament. It grows on a shrub or small tree. A large berry (the size of an orange), it is prized for its red pulp and seeds.

### POTATO (poh-TAY-toh) *vegetable*
The potato, native to the Andes mountains of Peru and Bolivia, is the world's most widely grown vegetable. Red- or brown-skinned, it is an underground tuber—a short, fleshy stem that has buds and can produce new plants. The sweet potato is the tuberous root of another plant, a tropical American vine.

### PUMPKIN (PUHMP-kin) *fruit/vegetable*
The pumpkin, probably a native of North America, grows on a vine. Some squashes are called pumpkins. Considered a vegetable by most people, it is really a fruit. In the United States, pumpkins are traditionally cooked into pies at Thanksgiving and carved into jack-o-lanterns at Halloween.

### Q QUINCE (kwinss) *fruit*
The quince is probably native to the Middle East. It can be found in Greek mythology. The applelike fruit grows on a small tree and is often used to make marmalade. The golden flesh becomes pinkish when cooked.

### R RADICCHIO (rah-DEEK-ee-oh) *vegetable*
Radicchio is a lettucelike plant native to Europe. Radicchio is the Italian name for chicory, and the plant is sometimes called red chicory. Some types are dark red with white veins.

### RADISH (RADD-ish) *vegetable*
The radish we know probably descended from a wild radish native to Europe and Asia. It is the pungent, edible root of a plant in the mustard family. It can be red, white, or black.

### RASPBERRY (RAZZ-behr-ee) *fruit*
The raspberry probably came from eastern Asia, where more than two hundred species are known. It grows on a bramble bush and is related to the rose. There are many types—red, purple, black, yellow, and white.

### RHUBARB (ROO-bahrb) *fruit/vegetable*
Rhubarb is native to cool parts of Asia, probably Tibet or Siberia. Although it is a vegetable, it is sometimes thought to be a fruit. The stalk is edible, but the leaf is poisonous. Also called pieplant, it is often baked in pies.

### RUTABAGA (roo-tah-BAY-gah) *vegetable*
The rutabaga, a species of turnip, originated in Europe or perhaps Asia. It grows underground and is an edible root. Usually golden inside, it is sometimes called Swedish turnip.

### S SPINACH (SPINN-ihch) *vegetable*
Spinach is native to southwestern Asia, probably Persia. Related to the beet, it has edible leaves. Fresh, uncooked spinach is popular in salads.

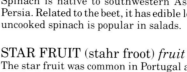
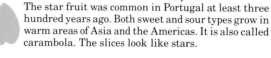

### STAR FRUIT (stahr froot) *fruit*
The star fruit was common in Portugal at least three hundred years ago. Both sweet and sour types grow in warm areas of Asia and the Americas. It is also called carambola. The slices look like stars.

### STRAWBERRY (STRAHW-behr-ee) *fruit*
The wild strawberry, known in ancient Rome, is native to temperate areas of the Northern Hemisphere. It grows on a low plant of the rose family.

### SWISS CHARD (swihss chahrd) *vegetable*
Swiss chard was known in the Mediterranean area more than two thousand years ago. Now it is grown throughout Europe, the United States, and South America. Although it is a type of beet, it is grown for its leaves and stems, not its roots.

### T TANGERINE (tann-jeh-REEN) *fruit*
The tangerine is native to southeastern Asia. It grows on a small tree and is related to the orange, but it is smaller, flatter, and has a loose rind so it is easier to peel. Sometimes it is called mandarin orange.

### TOMATO (toh-MAY-toh or toh-MAH-toh) *fruit/vegetable*
The tomato is native to South America. It is a fruit but is considered a vegetable. It grows on a plant and can be red or yellow. It was once thought to be poisonous.

### TURNIP (TUHR-nipp) *vegetable*
The turnip is native to prehistoric Europe and possibly Asia. It is the yellow or white root of a plant in the mustard family. Its leaves, called turnip greens, are edible as well.

### U UGLI FRUIT (UHG-lee fruit) *fruit*
Ugli fruit is thought to be native to the Far East and to Jamaica. It grows on a tree and is said to be a crossbreeding of the tangerine and the grapefruit. Jamaicans pronounce the name OOWG-lee.

### V VEGETABLE MARROW (VEHJ-tah-buhl MARR-oh) *fruit/vegetable*
Squash grew in Central America in prehistoric times. Vegetable marrow is a type of squash popular in Great Britain. A fruit that grows on a vinelike bush, it is considered a vegetable.

### W WATERCRESS (WAH-tuhr-kress) *vegetable*
Watercress, probably native to Europe and Asia Minor, was known four thousand years ago. A pungent mustard plant with edible leaves and stems, it grows in ponds and streams.

### WATERMELON (WAH-turh-mehl-uhn) *fruit*
Watermelon, native to Africa, has been known for four thousand years and is now grown worldwide. It is an oblong or round gourd that grows on a vine and has pink, red, or yellow flesh.

### X XIGUA (she-gwah) *fruit*
Xigua is the Chinese name for watermelon. The seeds are sometimes dried like pumpkin seeds, then cracked open and the centers eaten.

### Y YAM (yamm) *vegetable*
In the United States, an orange-fleshed sweet potato is called a yam. The true yam, native to warm areas of Africa and the Orient, is a large, starchy tuberous root. It is eaten like a potato.

### Z ZUCCHINI (zoo-KEE-nee) *fruit/vegetable*
Zucchini is one popular type of summer squash. Squash was cultivated in Mexico nearly nine thousand years ago. Zucchini is an Italian name that means "little squashes." Zucchini grows on a vinelike bush and is another fruit often considered a vegetable.

*It is difficult to find precise records of where certain fruits and vegetables were first grown. Long ago, as people traveled, they took along their favorite fruits and vegetables and exchanged them for other things, including foods that were new and different. Christopher Columbus, for example, brought corn to Europe from his first voyage to the West Indies. Fruits and vegetables spread to many areas of the world, and today they are grown across the globe and quickly shipped to markets in faraway places. That is why you don't always have to wait for a certain growing season to find your favorites. You can eat strawberries while you watch snowflakes falling outside your window. And someone, somewhere, is probably growing fruits and vegetables for you right now—so you can eat the alphabet any time.*